Laura Marano

by **Sarah Tieck**

Big Buddy Books

An Imprint of Abdo Publishing
www.abdopublishing.com

www.abdopublishing.com

Published by Abdo Publishing, a division of ABDO, PO Box 398166, Minneapolis, Minnesota 55439.
Copyright © 2015 by Abdo Consulting Group, Inc. International copyrights reserved in all countries. No part
of this book may be reproduced in any form without written permission from the publisher. Big Buddy Books™
is a trademark and logo of Abdo Publishing.

Printed in the United States of America, North Mankato, Minnesota.
092014
012015

THIS BOOK CONTAINS
RECYCLED MATERIALS

Cover Photo: Getty Images.
Interior Photos: Associated Press (p. 19); Disney Channel via Getty Images (pp. 14, 17, 21, 23); FilmMagic (p. 29);
    Getty Images (p. 25); Getty Images for Disney (p. 14); Getty Images for UNICEF (p. 27); Jordan Strauss/Invision/
    AP (p. 7); Warner Bros./Getty Images (p. 13); Miles Willis/Invision/AP (p. 17); WireImage (pp. 5, 9, 11).

Coordinating Series Editor: Rochelle Baltzer
Contributing Editors: Bridget O'Brien, Marcia Zappa
Graphic Design: Maria Hosley

Library of Congress Cataloging-in-Publication Data

Tieck, Sarah, 1976-
  Laura Marano : famous actress & singer / Sarah Tieck.
    pages cm. -- (Big buddy biographies)
  ISBN 978-1-62403-570-8
1. Marano, Laura, 1995---Juvenile literature. 2. Actors--United States--Biography--Juvenile literature. I. Title.
  PN2287.M44T54 2015
  791.4302'8092--dc23
  [B]
                     2014026416

Contents

Laura often attends media events as part of her work.

Rising Star

Laura Marano is an actress, singer, and songwriter. She has appeared in television shows and movies. Laura is known for starring in *Austin & Ally*.

Oregon

California   Nevada

PACIFIC OCEAN

Arizona

Los Angeles

MEXICO

Family Ties

Laura Marie Marano was born in Los Angeles, California, on November 29, 1995. Her parents are Damiano and Ellen Marano. Her older sister is Vanessa.

Laura and Vanessa are both actresses!

Theater Fan

When Laura was five, she began acting in a community theater. She acted at the Agoura Children's Theatre. This helped her build her skills as an actress.

When she was young, Laura attended rehearsals, shows, and events. This helped her understand the world of acting.

Lights! Camera! Action!

Young Laura knew she wanted to be an actress. So, she tried out for **professional** acting parts. She appeared in national **commercials** for businesses such as Gap. Laura also got small **roles** in popular television shows and movies.

As Laura's acting career began, people took notice of her skill.

For some of Laura's **roles**, she appeared in just one or two **episodes** of a television show. Other times, she'd have **recurring** roles over many years. Each one helped her become a better actress.

Laura appeared in the television show *Without a Trace*. She did voice work for *Ice Age: The Meltdown*. Laura also acted in *Ghost Whisperer*, *Back to You*, and *True Jackson, VP*.

Starting in 2003, Laura and Vanessa played sisters on *Without a Trace*. This show is about the FBI looking for missing people.

Laura and Ross are
friends on and off-screen.

Did you know...

Laura continued to attend high school while she built her acting career. Her friends were helpful and believed in her.

Big Break

Soon, Laura got a major **role** on a new television show for kids. In 2011, she began starring in *Austin & Ally*! This was an important step in her acting **career**.

On the show, Laura plays Ally Dawson. Ally is a shy songwriter. She is paired up with a bold singer named Austin. Austin is played by actor Ross Lynch.

Austin & Ally

Austin & Ally is a popular show on the Disney Channel. It is about Austin Moon and Ally Dawson. They live in Miami, Florida. These teens team up to make **pop** music.

Austin and Ally share adventures with their friends Dez and Trish. Sometimes, they run into trouble trying to make music. But they work together to reach their dreams.

In 2014, *Austin & Ally* was renewed for a fourth season.

On the show, Ally has stage fright. But in 2013, she performs alone for the first time.

New Opportunities

Because of her **role** on *Austin & Ally*, many people noticed Laura's talent. Soon, she had more chances to act. She did voice work for the cartoon *Fish Hooks*.

In 2014, Laura got a lead role in a movie called *A Sort of Homecoming*. It was about high school **debate**. Laura was excited to have a lead role in a film!

Laura's work has earned her invitations to red carpet events.

Songwriter

Laura has built a strong career. But aside from being an actress, she is a talented singer and songwriter. Laura spends time writing and recording songs. Sometimes, she practices performing them.

Just like her character on *Austin & Ally*, Laura enjoys writing songs. She especially likes to write pop songs for the piano.

An Actress's Life

As an actress, Laura is very busy. She must practice lines for her **roles**. During filming, she works on a **set** for several hours each day.

MOVIE SCREENINGS

ZALIENS 3: BRAIN EATERS FROM BEYOND   RISE OF THE ZALIEN
ZALIENS: THE RESISTANCE   ZALIENS 5
ZALIENS: FIRST STRIKE   THE ZALIENS II: DON'T BE AFRAID OF THE DARK

Laura's work requires her to wear makeup and costumes.

23

Laura's talents as an actress and a
singer have made her popular. She
has many fans! Laura appears in
magazines. She also talks to reporters
for news stories.

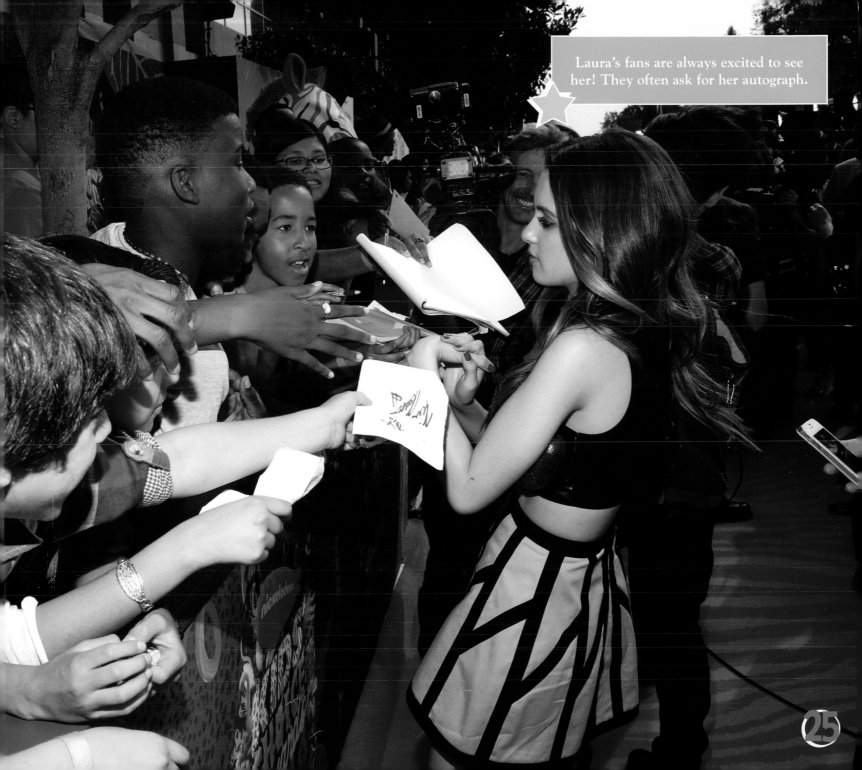

Laura's fans are always excited to see her! They often ask for her autograph.

Off the Screen

Laura spends free time with her family and friends. She likes to eat home-cooked meals with her family. She also enjoys playing piano and learning new things.

Laura likes to help others. She raises money for groups that care for children, such as UNICEF. She also supports **charities** that help animals.

In 2013, Laura visited a school as part of Trick-or-Treat for UNICEF.

Buzz

Laura's opportunities continue to grow. In 2014, she began working with Leigh-Allyn Baker on *Bad Hair Day*. They will star in this television movie.

Fans look forward to more from Laura Marano. Many believe she has a bright **future**!

In 2014, Laura graduated from high school.

Snapshot

★**Name**: Laura Marie Marano

★**Birthday**: November 29, 1995

★**Birthplace**: Los Angeles, California

★**Appearances**: *Without a Trace, Ice Age: The Meltdown, Ghost Whisperer, Back to You, True Jackson, VP, Austin & Ally, Fish Hooks, A Sort of Homecoming, Bad Hair Day*

Important Words

career work a person does to earn money for living.

charity a group or a fund that helps people in need.

commercial (kuh-MUHR-shuhl) a short message on television or radio that helps sell a product.

debate a planned discussion or argument about a question or topic, often held in public.

episode one show in a series of shows.

future (FYOO-chuhr) a time that has not yet occurred.

perform to do something in front of an audience.

pop relating to popular music.

professional (pruh-FEHSH-nuhl) working for money rather than only for pleasure.

recurring happening more than once.

role a part an actor plays.

set the place where a movie or a television show is recorded.

Websites

To learn more about Big Buddy Biographies, visit **booklinks.abdopublishing.com**. These links are routinely monitored and updated to provide the most current information available.

Index